Contents

Introduction 4
    What is Adult ADHD and why is it important to take charge of it? 5
    Symptoms and Diagnosis 6
    Dispelling myths and misconceptions about Adult ADHD 6
    How this book can help 8
Understanding Adult ADHD 9
    The history of Adult ADHD 10
    The science of Adult ADHD 11
    The different types of Adult ADHD 12
    The comorbidity of Adult ADHD and other mental health conditions 14
    The impact of Adult ADHD on daily life 15
Diagnosis and Evaluation 16
    The diagnosis process for Adult ADHD 16
    The criteria for diagnosing Adult ADHD 17
    Other tests and assessments used in diagnosing Adult ADHD 18
    The importance of a comprehensive evaluation 20
    How to prepare for an evaluation 21
    Medication and Other Treatments 22
    Medication options for Adult ADHD 23
    How medication works 24
    Alternative treatments for Adult ADHD 25
    Complementary treatments and therapies 26

- Developing a personalized treatment plan more organize way 27

Coping Strategies for Adult ADHD 29
- Strategies for coping with inattention and distractibility 29
- Strategies for coping with impulsivity and hyperactivity 30
- Time-management strategies 31
- Organizational strategies 32
- Coping with emotions and stress 33

Strategies for Personal Growth and Development 34
- Building self-awareness and self-acceptance 34
- Leveraging strengths and interests 35
- Developing new skills and habits 36
- Strategies for building relationships 37
- Mindfulness and self-care 38

Coping with Work and School 40
- Strategies for success in the workplace 40
- Navigating career challenges with Adult ADHD 41
- Strategies for academic success with Adult ADHD 43
- Managing ADHD in college and graduate school 44
- Accommodations and resources for Adult ADHD in the workplace and academic settings 46

Building Strong Relationships and Support Networks 48
- Communicating about Adult ADHD with loved ones 49
- Building supportive relationships 50
- Joining support groups 51
- Strategies for managing conflict 52
- Coping with social anxiety 53

Navigating Life Transitions and Challenges 54
ADHD and life transitions 54
Managing ADHD during major life changes 55
Coping with co-occurring disorders......................57
Coping with financial challenges..........................58
Planning for the future with Adult ADHD............59
Living Your Best Life with Adult ADHD 61
Celebrating successes...61
Strategies for maintaining progress......................62
Living with intention and purpose 63
Staying engaged and motivated 64
Continuing to grow and learn...............................65
Resources for Adult ADHD..67
Books and websites...68
Organizations and support groups.......................70
Professional help and treatment options 71
Apps and tools for managing Adult ADHD..........72
Additional resources for Adult ADHD 74
Conclusion 75
Recap of key concepts 75
The importance of taking charge of Adult ADHD.................76

INTRODUCTION

Attention Deficit Hyperactivity Disorder (ADHD) is a neurodevelopmental disorder that affects individuals across the lifespan, including adults. It is characterized by symptoms of inattention, hyperactivity, and impulsivity, and can significantly impact an individual's daily life, relationships, and career. Despite its prevalence and impact, many individuals with Adult ADHD are not diagnosed or treated properly, leading to ongoing challenges and frustrations.

This book aims to provide a comprehensive guide for adults with ADHD who want to take charge of their lives and thrive. Whether you've been recently diagnosed or have been living with ADHD for years, this book offers evidence-based strategies and practical tips to help you manage your symptoms, improve your relationships, and achieve your goals.

With a focus on empowerment and personal growth, this book covers everything from diagnosis and evaluation to medication and other treatments, coping strategies, building strong relationships and support networks, navigating work and school, and planning for the future. Through engaging anecdotes, real-life success stories, and practical advice, this book offers readers the tools they need to overcome challenges and build fulfilling lives with ADHD.

Whether you're looking to manage symptoms, build resilience, or achieve your full potential, this book is a valuable resource for anyone seeking to take charge of their Adult ADHD and thrive.

WHAT IS ADULT ADHD AND WHY IS IT IMPORTANT TO TAKE CHARGE OF IT?

Attention-deficit/hyperactivity disorder (ADHD) is a neurodevelopmental disorder that can affect individuals of all ages. The prevalence of ADHD in adults varies depending on the source, the diagnostic criteria used, and the population being studied.

According to the Diagnostic and Statistical Manual of Mental Disorders, Fifth Edition (DSM-5), the prevalence of ADHD in adults is estimated to be around 2.5% to 4.4% in the general population. However, other studies have reported higher rates of ADHD in adults, ranging from 4% to 5% to as high as 8%.

Some studies suggest that ADHD may be underdiagnosed in adults, particularly in women and individuals with milder symptoms. It is also important to note that ADHD can often co-occur with other mental health conditions, such as anxiety and depression, which can complicate the diagnosis and treatment of ADHD in adults.

While the exact prevalence of ADHD in adults remains a topic of debate, it is clear that ADHD can have significant impacts on daily functioning and quality of life for those who experience it, and early diagnosis and treatment can be key to improving outcomes.

SYMPTOMS AND DIAGNOSIS

Symptoms are the subjective experiences that a person has and reports, such as pain, fatigue, or dizziness. Symptoms can be caused by a variety of factors, including illness, injury, or psychological distress.

Diagnosis is the process of identifying the underlying cause of a person's symptoms. It involves gathering information about the person's medical history, conducting a physical examination, and sometimes ordering tests, such as blood tests, imaging studies, or biopsies.

The diagnosis of a medical condition can be challenging and often requires the expertise of a healthcare professional, such as a doctor or specialist. In some cases, multiple tests may be needed, or a referral to a specialist may be necessary.

It's important to seek medical attention if you are experiencing symptoms, as early diagnosis and treatment can lead to better outcomes.

DISPELLING MYTHS AND MISCONCEPTIONS ABOUT ADULT ADHD

There are several common myths and misconceptions about Adult ADHD that can create misunderstandings and stigma. Here are some of the most common myths and the truths that dispel them:

Myth: ADHD only affects children and is outgrown in adulthood.

Truth: ADHD is a neurodevelopmental disorder that often persists into adulthood. In fact, it is estimated that up to 60% of children with ADHD will continue to have symptoms in adulthood.

Myth: ADHD is caused by bad parenting or a lack of discipline.
Truth: ADHD is a neurobiological disorder with genetic and environmental factors. It is not caused by poor parenting or a lack of discipline.

Myth: ADHD is not a real disorder, and people with ADHD are just lazy or unmotivated.

Truth: ADHD is a real medical condition that is recognized by major medical and psychiatric organizations, including the American Psychiatric Association and the World Health Organization. People with ADHD often struggle with executive functioning skills, such as organization, time management, and self-regulation.

Myth: ADHD is over-diagnosed, and people with ADHD are just seeking medication to enhance performance.

Truth: While it is true that ADHD is sometimes over-diagnosed or misdiagnosed, it is important to recognize that ADHD can have a significant impact on daily life. People with ADHD may struggle with completing tasks, paying attention, and regulating their behavior, which can lead to problems in their personal and professional lives.

Myth: ADHD only affects boys and men.

Truth: While boys are more likely to be diagnosed with ADHD than girls, ADHD can affect people of any gender. Girls and women with ADHD may be less likely to be diagnosed because they may exhibit different symptoms than boys and men, such as inattentiveness instead of hyperactivity.

Dispelling these myths and misconceptions is important because it helps people with ADHD receive the understanding, support, and treatment they need to manage their symptoms and lead fulfilling lives. By recognizing ADHD as a real and legitimate condition, we can help reduce stigma and create a more supportive environment for people with ADHD.

HOW THIS BOOK CAN HELP

This book on taking charge of Adult ADHD can help in several ways:

- **Understanding Adult ADHD:** The book can help individuals understand the nature of Adult ADHD, the symptoms they may experience, and how ADHD can impact their daily lives. By gaining a better understanding of their condition, individuals can feel empowered to take action to manage their symptoms.
- **Diagnosis:** The book can provide information on how to seek a proper diagnosis of Adult ADHD, including the different assessment tools and diagnostic criteria used by healthcare professionals.
- **Treatment Options:** The book can provide information on various treatment options available for Adult ADHD, including medication, therapy, and lifestyle changes. It can help individuals understand the benefits and drawbacks of each treatment option and work with their healthcare provider to develop an individualized treatment plan.
- **Coping Strategies:** The book can provide practical strategies for managing ADHD symptoms, such as organization, time management, and self-regulation. These strategies can help individuals develop the skills they need to overcome the challenges of ADHD and improve their daily functioning.
- **Building Support Networks:** The book can provide guidance on building a support network of family, friends, and professionals who can provide support and encouragement to individuals with Adult ADHD. It can also provide information on support groups and online communities where individuals with ADHD can connect with others who share similar experiences.

Overall, this book can help individuals with Adult ADHD take charge of their condition, learn to manage their symptoms, and improve their quality of life. By providing accurate information, practical strategies, and support, this book can empower individuals with Adult ADHD to live fulfilling lives despite their condition.

UNDERSTANDING ADULT ADHD

Understanding Adult ADHD is an important first step in taking charge of the condition. Here are some key aspects of Adult ADHD that individuals should understand:

1. Symptoms: Adult ADHD symptoms can be categorized into two types: inattentive and hyperactive-impulsive. Inattentive symptoms may include difficulty with focus, forgetfulness, and disorganization, while hyperactive-impulsive symptoms may include restlessness, impulsivity, and interrupting others.
2. Causes: The exact causes of Adult ADHD are not fully understood, but research suggests that genetics, brain structure and function, and environmental factors may all play a role.
3. Diagnosis: A proper diagnosis of Adult ADHD requires a comprehensive evaluation by a healthcare professional, such as a psychiatrist or psychologist. The evaluation may include interviews, questionnaires, and behavioral observations.
4. Co-occurring conditions: Individuals with Adult ADHD may also have co-occurring conditions, such as anxiety, depression, or substance use disorders. It is important to identify and treat these conditions alongside ADHD to improve overall functioning.
5. Impact on daily life: Adult ADHD can have a significant impact on daily life, including academic and occupational performance, relationships, and self-esteem.

Understanding how ADHD affects daily life can help individuals identify areas where they need support and develop strategies for managing their symptoms.
6. Treatment options: There are various treatment options available for Adult ADHD, including medication, therapy, and lifestyle changes. It is important for individuals to work with their healthcare provider to develop an individualized treatment plan that addresses their unique needs and preferences.

Understanding Adult ADHD is an important step in taking charge of the condition. By gaining a better understanding of the symptoms, causes, diagnosis, impact on daily life, and treatment options, individuals with Adult ADHD can develop a personalized plan for managing their symptoms and improving their quality of life.

THE HISTORY OF ADULT ADHD

The history of adult ADHD is relatively recent, as ADHD was originally believed to be a childhood disorder. It wasn't until the 1980s and 1990s that researchers began to recognize that many individuals with ADHD continue to experience symptoms well into adulthood.

In 1980, the American Psychiatric Association (APA) first included ADHD in the third edition of the Diagnostic and Statistical Manual of Mental Disorders (DSM-III). However, the diagnostic criteria were largely based on studies of children, and there was little consideration of ADHD in adults.

In 1994, the APA revised the diagnostic criteria for ADHD in the fourth edition of the DSM (DSM-IV), which included specific diagnostic criteria for adults. The revision acknowledged that ADHD is a chronic disorder that can persist into adulthood and recognized the importance of considering adult symptoms and impairments in the diagnosis and treatment of the disorder.

Since then, there has been growing recognition and awareness of adult ADHD, leading to increased research and treatment options for adults with the disorder. In 2013, the APA released the fifth edition of the DSM (DSM-5), which further refined the diagnostic criteria for adult ADHD and emphasized the need for a comprehensive evaluation of symptoms and impairments across different settings and domains.

Overall, the history of adult ADHD has been marked by a gradual recognition of the disorder as a significant and often lifelong condition that can have a significant impact on daily functioning and quality of life for those who experience it.

THE SCIENCE OF ADULT ADHD

Adult ADHD (Attention Deficit Hyperactivity Disorder) is a neurodevelopmental disorder characterized by symptoms of inattention, hyperactivity, and impulsivity that persist into adulthood. The science of Adult ADHD involves studying the underlying causes, risk factors, and effective treatments for the condition.

Research has shown that ADHD has a strong genetic component, with certain genes being associated with an increased risk of developing the disorder. Environmental factors, such as prenatal exposure to tobacco smoke or alcohol, may also increase the risk of developing ADHD.

Brain imaging studies have found differences in the structure and function of the brains of people with ADHD compared to those without the condition. For example, people with ADHD may have differences in the size and activity of certain brain regions involved in attention, impulse control, and decision-making.

There are several effective treatments for Adult ADHD, including medications such as stimulants and non-stimulants, as well as behavioral therapy and lifestyle changes. These treatments can help manage the symptoms of ADHD and improve overall functioning and quality of life.

Ongoing research is needed to better understand the complex nature of Adult ADHD and to develop more targeted and effective treatments.

THE DIFFERENT TYPES OF ADULT ADHD

Understanding Adult ADHD is an important first step in taking charge of the condition. Here are some key aspects of Adult ADHD that individuals should understand:

Predominantly Inattentive Presentation: This subtype of Adult ADHD is characterized by symptoms of inattention. Individuals with this subtype may struggle with focus, forgetfulness, and disorganization. They may have difficulty completing tasks, following through on instructions, and maintaining attention during conversations. Some common symptoms of predominantly inattentive presentation include:

- Difficulty paying attention to details and making careless mistakes
- Difficulty sustaining attention during tasks or activities
- Forgetfulness and losing things necessary for tasks or activities
- Avoiding or disliking tasks that require sustained mental effort
- Disorganization and difficulty with time management

Predominantly Hyperactive-Impulsive Presentation: This subtype of Adult ADHD is characterized by symptoms of hyperactivity and impulsivity. Individuals with this subtype may struggle with restlessness, fidgeting, interrupting others, and impulsive decision-making. Some common symptoms of predominantly hyperactive-impulsive presentation include:

- Fidgeting and restlessness
- Interrupting others or speaking out of turn
- Difficulty waiting their turn
- Impulsive decision-making

- Engaging in risky behaviors without thinking through the consequences

Combined Presentation: This subtype of Adult ADHD is characterized by a combination of inattentive, hyperactive, and impulsive symptoms. Individuals with this subtype may experience symptoms from both the inattentive and hyperactive-impulsive subtypes, such as difficulty with focus and restlessness. Some common symptoms of combined presentation include:

- Difficulty with focus and attention
- Fidgeting and restlessness
- Interrupting others or speaking out of turn
- Difficulty waiting their turn
- Impulsive decision-making

It is important to note that not all individuals with Adult ADHD fit neatly into one of these subtypes. Some individuals may experience symptoms that do not fit into any one subtype or may experience symptoms from more than one subtype. Additionally, Adult ADHD symptoms can vary in severity and may change over time. It is important for individuals to work with a healthcare provider to develop a personalized treatment plan that addresses their unique symptoms and needs.

THE COMORBIDITY OF ADULT ADHD AND OTHER MENTAL HEALTH CONDITIONS

ADHD often co-occurs with other mental health conditions, which can complicate diagnosis and treatment. Here are some of the most commonly reported comorbid conditions in adults with ADHD:

1. **Anxiety disorders:** Studies suggest that around 30-40% of adults with ADHD also have an anxiety disorder, such as generalized anxiety disorder, social anxiety disorder, or panic disorder. The symptoms of ADHD, such as restlessness, distractibility, and impulsivity, can exacerbate anxiety symptoms and vice versa.
2. **Mood disorders:** Depression and bipolar disorder are also common comorbidities in adults with ADHD. The risk of developing a mood disorder is higher in individuals with ADHD compared to the general population, and symptoms of ADHD can often mask or mimic symptoms of depression or bipolar disorder.
3. **Substance use disorders:** ADHD is a risk factor for the development of substance use disorders, particularly in individuals who struggle with impulse control and emotional regulation. Studies suggest that around 20-30% of adults with ADHD also have a substance use disorder.
4. **Personality disorders:** Some research has found that individuals with ADHD are at increased risk for certain personality disorders, such as borderline personality disorder and antisocial personality disorder. However, the relationship between ADHD and personality disorders is complex and not fully understood.
5. **Sleep disorders:** Sleep problems are common in individuals with ADHD, and can exacerbate symptoms of the disorder. Additionally, untreated ADHD can contribute to sleep problems, creating a cycle of symptoms.

THE IMPACT OF ADULT ADHD ON DAILY LIFE

Adult ADHD (Attention Deficit Hyperactivity Disorder) can have a significant impact on daily life in a number of ways. Some common ways that Adult ADHD can affect daily life include:

1. **Work performance:** Adults with ADHD may have difficulty with time management, organization, and completing tasks on time. They may also struggle with staying focused and maintaining attention, leading to decreased productivity and performance at work.
2. **Relationships:** ADHD can make it difficult for adults to pay attention and listen to others, leading to communication difficulties and relationship problems. Adults with ADHD may also struggle with impulse control, leading to impulsive behavior or saying things without thinking, which can negatively impact relationships.
3. **Emotional regulation:** Adults with ADHD may struggle with regulating their emotions, leading to mood swings, anger outbursts, and irritability. They may also have difficulty managing stress and anxiety.
4. **Financial management:** Adults with ADHD may have difficulty with financial management, including paying bills on time, budgeting, and saving money. They may also struggle with impulse control when it comes to spending money.
5. **Daily routines:** Adults with ADHD may have difficulty with establishing and maintaining daily routines, such as sleeping and eating habits. They may struggle with initiating tasks, leading to procrastination and difficulty with completing daily tasks.

These challenges can lead to a range of negative outcomes, including financial problems, job loss, social isolation, and low self-esteem. However, with proper diagnosis and treatment, individuals with Adult ADHD can learn strategies to manage their symptoms and improve their daily functioning. Treatment options include medication, therapy, and lifestyle changes, such as exercise and mindfulness practices.

DIAGNOSIS AND EVALUATION

In this chapter, we will explore the important topic of diagnosis and evaluation of Adult ADHD. We will delve into the various methods and tools used by healthcare professionals to assess and diagnose the disorder, as well as discuss the importance of seeking an accurate diagnosis. Additionally, we will explore the potential benefits and challenges of receiving a diagnosis, and the impact it can have on an individual's life. Finally, we will examine some common misconceptions and myths about ADHD diagnosis and provide guidance on how to seek appropriate evaluation and diagnosis.

THE DIAGNOSIS PROCESS FOR ADULT ADHD

The diagnosis process for Adult ADHD typically involves a comprehensive evaluation by a healthcare professional, such as a psychologist, psychiatrist, or primary care physician. Here are some common steps in the diagnosis process:

1. Initial Screening: The healthcare professional will begin with an initial screening to gather information about the individual's symptoms and history. This may include a self-assessment questionnaire, a review of medical records, and interviews with family members or other people who know the individual well.
2. Diagnostic Criteria: To receive a diagnosis of Adult ADHD, an individual must meet specific criteria outlined in the Diagnostic and Statistical Manual of Mental Disorders (DSM). The healthcare professional will use the DSM criteria to determine if the individual's symptoms meet the criteria for a diagnosis.
3. Comprehensive Evaluation: If the initial screening suggests that Adult ADHD may be present, the healthcare professional will conduct a more comprehensive

evaluation. This may include psychological testing, a medical exam, and a review of the individual's history of symptoms and behaviors.
4. Differential Diagnosis: The healthcare professional will also consider other conditions that may be contributing to the individual's symptoms, such as depression, anxiety, or sleep disorders. This is known as a differential diagnosis and is an important step in ensuring an accurate diagnosis.
5. Feedback and Recommendations: Once the evaluation is complete, the healthcare professional will provide feedback on the diagnosis and recommendations for treatment. This may include medication, therapy, lifestyle changes, or a combination of these approaches.

THE CRITERIA FOR DIAGNOSING ADULT ADHD

Diagnosing adult ADHD involves a comprehensive evaluation of symptoms, impairments, and functional difficulties across different settings and domains. The diagnostic criteria for adult ADHD are outlined in the Diagnostic and Statistical Manual of Mental Disorders, Fifth Edition (DSM-5), and involve the following steps:

1. Symptom assessment: The first step in diagnosing ADHD in adults is to assess the presence and severity of ADHD symptoms. The DSM-5 specifies two main symptom clusters: inattention and hyperactivity/impulsivity. These symptoms must have persisted for at least six months, be present before age 12, and be present in two or more settings (e.g., work and home).
2. Impairment assessment: The presence of ADHD symptoms alone is not sufficient for a diagnosis. The symptoms must also be associated with significant impairment or distress in one or more areas of functioning, such as work, school, social relationships, or daily activities.

3. Rule out other conditions: Before diagnosing ADHD, other medical or psychiatric conditions that may be contributing to the symptoms must be ruled out or addressed. For example, symptoms of ADHD can be similar to those of anxiety, depression, bipolar disorder, or sleep disorders.
4. History and documentation: A thorough history of the individual's symptoms and impairments is essential for an accurate diagnosis. This may involve a review of medical records, previous assessments or evaluations, and interviews with family members or other significant individuals who have observed the individual's behavior.
5. Differential diagnosis: Finally, a comprehensive assessment should include a differential diagnosis, which considers other conditions that may share similar symptoms with ADHD. For example, anxiety or depression can manifest as difficulty concentrating or low motivation, but may require different treatment approaches.

OTHER TESTS AND ASSESSMENTS USED IN DIAGNOSING ADULT ADHD

Diagnosing Adult ADHD (Attention Deficit Hyperactivity Disorder) requires a comprehensive evaluation that includes a variety of tests and assessments. Here are some of the commonly used assessments:

1. Diagnostic and Statistical Manual of Mental Disorders (DSM): The DSM is a diagnostic tool used by mental health professionals to identify and diagnose mental health disorders, including ADHD. The most recent edition, DSM-5, outlines the criteria for diagnosing ADHD based on symptoms and severity.
2. Clinical Interviews: Clinical interviews are used to gather information about an individual's medical history, symptoms, and current functioning. The clinician may ask

about childhood behavior, current symptoms, and daily functioning to help assess for ADHD.
3. Rating Scales: Rating scales are questionnaires that are used to gather information about an individual's symptoms and behaviors. They may be completed by the individual, their family members, or other individuals who are familiar with the individual's behavior, such as teachers or coworkers. Common rating scales used to assess for ADHD include the Conners Adult ADHD Rating Scale and the ADHD Rating Scale-IV.
4. Cognitive Tests: Cognitive tests, such as the Continuous Performance Test (CPT) and the Stroop Test, may be used to assess for ADHD by measuring attention, impulsivity, and response inhibition.
5. Medical and Neurological Evaluation: A medical and neurological evaluation may be done to rule out other medical conditions that can mimic ADHD, such as thyroid disorders or sleep disorders. A physical exam, blood tests, and imaging studies may be used in this evaluation.

The diagnosis of Adult ADHD requires a comprehensive evaluation that takes into account multiple sources of information. This evaluation can help to rule out other potential causes of symptoms and ensure that the diagnosis is accurate.

THE IMPORTANCE OF A COMPREHENSIVE EVALUATION

A comprehensive evaluation is critical in accurately diagnosing Adult ADHD because the disorder can be difficult to diagnose and symptoms can overlap with other conditions. Here are some reasons why a comprehensive evaluation is so important:

1. Accuracy: A comprehensive evaluation helps to ensure an accurate diagnosis by ruling out other conditions that may have similar symptoms, such as anxiety or depression. This helps to prevent misdiagnosis and ensures that individuals receive the appropriate treatment.
2. Understanding Severity: A comprehensive evaluation can also help to determine the severity of the individual's symptoms, which is important in developing an effective treatment plan. This includes identifying any comorbid conditions, such as substance abuse or learning disabilities, which can complicate the diagnosis and treatment of Adult ADHD.
3. Identifying Contributing Factors: A comprehensive evaluation can also help to identify contributing factors that may be exacerbating the individual's symptoms, such as sleep disorders or high levels of stress. By addressing these factors, the healthcare professional can help to improve the individual's overall functioning and quality of life.
4. Tailoring Treatment: Finally, a comprehensive evaluation can help to tailor the treatment approach to the individual's unique needs. This may include medication, therapy, lifestyle changes, or a combination of these approaches. By developing a personalized treatment plan, the healthcare professional can help the individual achieve optimal outcomes and improve their overall well-being.

HOW TO PREPARE FOR AN EVALUATION

Preparing for an evaluation for Adult ADHD can help ensure that the process is as thorough and accurate as possible. Here are some tips on how to prepare for an evaluation:

1. **Gather Information:**
   Before the evaluation, gather any relevant information about your symptoms, such as how long you have been experiencing them, when they occur, and how they affect your daily life. It may also be helpful to gather information about your family history, medical history, and any medications or supplements you are taking.
2. **Fill out Self-Assessment Questionnaires:**
   Many healthcare professionals use self-assessment questionnaires to help diagnose Adult ADHD. Fill out any questionnaires provided by your healthcare professional before the evaluation. This will help the healthcare professional understand your symptoms and give them a baseline for assessing your condition.
3. **Bring a List of Questions:**
   Before the evaluation, write down any questions you have about Adult ADHD or the evaluation process. This can help you feel more prepared and ensure that you get the information you need.
4. **Bring Support:**
   It can be helpful to bring a family member or close friend with you to the evaluation. They can provide additional information about your symptoms and help you feel more comfortable during the evaluation process.
5. **Be Honest:**
   During the evaluation, be honest about your symptoms, even if you feel embarrassed or uncomfortable. The healthcare professional is there to help you, and they need accurate information to make an accurate diagnosis and develop an effective treatment plan.
6. **Follow Instructions:**

Finally, be sure to follow any instructions provided by your healthcare professional before the evaluation, such as fasting or avoiding certain medications. This can help ensure that the evaluation is as accurate as possible.

MEDICATION AND OTHER TREATMENTS

Medication and other treatments can be effective in managing the symptoms of Adult ADHD. Here is an overview of the different types of medication and other treatments that may be recommended for Adult ADHD:

- **Stimulant Medications:** Stimulant medications are the most commonly prescribed medications for Adult ADHD. They work by increasing levels of dopamine and norepinephrine in the brain, which can improve attention and focus. Examples of stimulant medications include methylphenidate (e.g., Ritalin) and amphetamine (e.g., Adderall).
- **Non-Stimulant Medications:** Non-stimulant medications are also used to treat Adult ADHD, particularly for those who do not respond well to stimulant medications. These medications work by increasing levels of norepinephrine in the brain. Examples of non-stimulant medications include atomoxetine (e.g., Strattera) and guanfacine (e.g., Intuniv).
- **Psychotherapy:** Psychotherapy, such as cognitive-behavioral therapy (CBT), can be helpful in managing the symptoms of Adult ADHD. CBT can help individuals with Adult ADHD develop coping strategies to manage their symptoms, improve their organizational skills, and reduce impulsivity.
- **Coaching:** Coaching can be beneficial for individuals with Adult ADHD who struggle with organization and time management. ADHD coaches can provide support and guidance in developing strategies to manage daily tasks, improve productivity, and achieve goals.

- **Lifestyle Changes:** Making lifestyle changes can also be helpful in managing the symptoms of Adult ADHD. This includes getting enough sleep, eating a healthy diet, and exercising regularly. These changes can help to reduce stress and improve overall well-being.
- **Alternative Treatments:** Some individuals with Adult ADHD may benefit from alternative treatments such as mindfulness meditation, yoga, or acupuncture. However, there is limited scientific evidence to support the effectiveness of these treatments in managing the symptoms of Adult ADHD.

MEDICATION OPTIONS FOR ADULT ADHD

There are several medications approved for the treatment of adult ADHD. These medications fall into two main categories: stimulants and non-stimulants. Here are some commonly prescribed medications for adult ADHD:

- **Stimulants:** Stimulant medications are the most commonly prescribed medications for ADHD. They work by increasing the levels of dopamine and norepinephrine in the brain, which can help improve attention, focus, and impulse control. Examples of stimulant medications include methylphenidate (e.g., Ritalin, Concerta), dextroamphetamine (e.g., Dexedrine), and mixed amphetamine salts (e.g., Adderall). These medications come in different forms, including short-acting, intermediate-acting, and long-acting formulations.
- **Non-stimulants:** Non-stimulant medications are an alternative for individuals who cannot tolerate or do not respond to stimulant medications. These medications work by targeting different neurotransmitters in the brain, such as norepinephrine and serotonin. Examples of non-stimulant medications for ADHD include atomoxetine (e.g., Strattera), guanfacine (e.g., Intuniv), and clonidine (e.g., Kapvay).

It's important to note that medication should always be prescribed and monitored by a qualified healthcare professional, as dosages and potential side effects can vary depending on the individual. Additionally, medication should be used in conjunction with other treatments for ADHD, such as therapy, lifestyle modifications, and organizational strategies, to optimize treatment outcomes.

Lastly, it's important to understand that medication is not a cure for ADHD, but can help manage symptoms and improve functioning. Regular check-ins with a healthcare provider and ongoing evaluation of the effectiveness of medication are essential for successful management of ADHD.

HOW MEDICATION WORKS

Medication is a common treatment option for Adult ADHD (Attention Deficit Hyperactivity Disorder). There are two main types of medication used to treat ADHD: stimulant medications and non-stimulant medications.

Stimulant medications, such as methylphenidate and amphetamines, work by increasing the levels of certain neurotransmitters in the brain, including dopamine and norepinephrine. These neurotransmitters play a key role in regulating attention, impulse control, and other executive functions. By increasing the levels of these neurotransmitters, stimulant medications can help to improve focus, attention, and overall functioning in individuals with ADHD.

Non-stimulant medications, such as atomoxetine and guanfacine, work by targeting different neurotransmitters in the brain. Atomoxetine is a selective norepinephrine reuptake inhibitor, which means that it increases the levels of norepinephrine in the brain. Guanfacine works by targeting the alpha-2A adrenergic receptor, which is involved in regulating attention and impulse control.

While medication can be effective in treating ADHD, it's important to note that medication is not a cure and does not address the underlying causes of ADHD. Medication should be used in combination with other treatments, such as therapy and lifestyle changes, to help individuals manage their symptoms and improve their overall functioning.

It's also important to work with a healthcare professional to determine the best medication and dosage for each individual, as the effectiveness and side effects of medication can vary depending on the person. Additionally, medication should be monitored closely and adjusted as needed to ensure optimal benefits and minimize potential side effects.

ALTERNATIVE TREATMENTS FOR ADULT ADHD

There are several alternative treatments that individuals with Adult ADHD may find helpful in managing their symptoms. However, it is important to note that the effectiveness of these treatments has not been extensively studied, and they should not be used as a substitute for evidence-based treatments such as medication and psychotherapy. Here are some alternative treatments that may be beneficial for Adult ADHD:

Mindfulness Meditation

Mindfulness meditation involves focusing on the present moment and accepting it without judgment. It has been shown to reduce stress and improve attention and cognitive flexibility, which may be helpful for individuals with Adult ADHD.

Yoga

Yoga is a mind-body practice that involves physical postures, breathing exercises, and meditation. It has been shown to reduce stress, improve mood, and increase focus and attention.

Acupuncture

Acupuncture involves inserting needles into specific points on the body to stimulate the flow of energy. It has been shown to reduce stress and improve attention and impulse control in individuals with ADHD.

Omega-3 Fatty Acids

Omega-3 fatty acids are essential fatty acids that are found in fish oil and some other foods. They have been shown to improve attention and cognitive function in individuals with ADHD.

Herbal Supplements

Some herbal supplements, such as ginkgo biloba and ginseng, have been suggested as possible treatments for Adult ADHD. However, there is limited scientific evidence to support their effectiveness.

COMPLEMENTARY TREATMENTS AND THERAPIES

In addition to medication, there are several complementary treatments and therapies that may be helpful for managing symptoms of adult ADHD. Here are some examples:

a) Cognitive Behavioral Therapy (CBT): CBT is a type of talk therapy that focuses on changing negative thoughts and behaviors that contribute to ADHD symptoms. It can help individuals with ADHD learn coping strategies for managing their symptoms, such as improving time management, organization, and problem-solving skills.
b) Mindfulness-Based Therapies: Mindfulness-based therapies, such as mindfulness meditation or yoga, can help improve attention, impulse control, and emotional regulation. These practices can also help reduce stress and anxiety, which can exacerbate ADHD symptoms.
c) Exercise: Regular physical activity can help improve executive functioning, such as attention, working memory, and cognitive flexibility. Exercise can also help

reduce symptoms of anxiety and depression, which are common in individuals with ADHD.
d) Nutrition: A balanced diet with adequate protein, complex carbohydrates, and healthy fats can help stabilize blood sugar levels and improve focus and attention. Additionally, some research suggests that omega-3 fatty acids, found in fatty fish and supplements, may be helpful for reducing symptoms of ADHD.
e) Coaching: ADHD coaching can be helpful for individuals who need support and guidance in developing practical strategies for managing their symptoms. ADHD coaches can provide assistance with organizational skills, time management, and goal-setting.

DEVELOPING A PERSONALIZED TREATMENT PLAN MORE ORGANIZE WAY

Developing a personalized treatment plan for Adult ADHD (Attention Deficit Hyperactivity Disorder) requires a comprehensive evaluation and a collaborative approach between the individual, their healthcare provider, and other members of their care team. Here are some steps to help develop a personalized treatment plan:

1. Assessment: A thorough assessment should be conducted to evaluate the individual's symptoms, medical history, and daily functioning. This may include clinical interviews, rating scales, cognitive tests, medical and neurological evaluations, and input from family members, friends, and other care providers.
2. Goal Setting: Based on the assessment, the individual and their healthcare provider can work together to set treatment goals that are specific, measurable, achievable, relevant, and time-bound (SMART). These goals should take into account the individual's unique needs, challenges, and strengths.
3. Treatment Options: Once goals have been established, the healthcare provider can present a range of treatment

options based on the individual's symptoms and preferences. These may include medication, therapy, and lifestyle changes such as exercise, diet, and mindfulness practices. The provider can discuss the benefits, risks, and potential side effects of each treatment option to help the individual make an informed decision.
4. Treatment Plan: A personalized treatment plan should be developed based on the individual's goals, treatment options, and preferences. This plan should include the type and dosage of medication, the frequency and duration of therapy sessions, and specific lifestyle changes that will be made. The plan should be reviewed and updated regularly to ensure that it is effective and sustainable.
5. Support: The individual may need ongoing support from their healthcare provider, family members, friends, and other care providers to help them implement their treatment plan and achieve their goals. This may include regular check-ins, education and resources, and strategies for managing setbacks or challenges.

Developing a personalized treatment plan for Adult ADHD requires a comprehensive assessment, goal setting, collaboration with healthcare providers, consideration of treatment options, and ongoing support. A personalized treatment plan can help individuals manage their symptoms and improve their daily functioning, leading to improved quality of life.

COPING STRATEGIES FOR ADULT ADHD

Coping strategies are an important tool for individuals with Adult ADHD to manage their symptoms and improve their daily functioning. These strategies can help individuals to stay organized, reduce distractibility, and improve their ability to focus and complete tasks. Some common coping strategies for Adult ADHD include:

STRATEGIES FOR COPING WITH INATTENTION AND DISTRACTIBILITY

Coping with inattention and distractibility can be a challenge for individuals with Adult ADHD, but there are several strategies that can help. Here are some coping strategies that can be effective:

1. Minimizing distractions: Reducing distractions in the environment can help individuals with Adult ADHD to focus on the task at hand. This can be achieved by working in a quiet space, turning off electronic devices, and minimizing clutter.
2. Prioritizing tasks: It can be helpful to prioritize tasks based on their level of importance and urgency. This can help individuals with Adult ADHD to stay on track and reduce the likelihood of forgetting important tasks.
3. Using a timer: Setting a timer for a specific amount of time can help individuals with Adult ADHD to stay focused on a task. This technique is known as the Pomodoro Technique, and involves working on a task for a set amount of time (usually 25 minutes), taking a short break, and then resuming work.
4. Taking breaks: Taking short breaks can help individuals with Adult ADHD to recharge and refocus. This can

involve taking a walk, doing some stretching exercises, or simply taking a few minutes to relax.
5. Using mindfulness techniques: Mindfulness techniques such as deep breathing and meditation can help individuals with Adult ADHD to reduce stress and improve focus. These techniques involve focusing on the present moment and accepting it without judgment.

Coping with inattention and distractibility requires a multi-faceted approach that involves both environmental and behavioral strategies. It may take some trial and error to find the strategies that work best for each individual, but with persistence and patience, it is possible to manage these symptoms effectively.

STRATEGIES FOR COPING WITH IMPULSIVITY AND HYPERACTIVITY

Coping with impulsivity and hyperactivity can be challenging for individuals with Adult ADHD, but there are several strategies that can help. Here are some coping strategies that can be effective:

1. Engaging in physical activity: Physical exercise can help to reduce hyperactivity and impulsivity by channeling excess energy and increasing focus. Activities such as yoga, walking, or swimming can be particularly helpful.
2. Using positive self-talk: Positive self-talk can help individuals with Adult ADHD to stay calm and focused in the face of impulsive urges. This can involve reminding oneself of the consequences of impulsive actions and focusing on long-term goals.
3. Delaying gratification: Delaying gratification can help individuals with Adult ADHD to resist impulsive urges. This can involve setting goals and working towards them gradually, rather than seeking immediate rewards.
4. Using relaxation techniques: Relaxation techniques such as deep breathing, meditation, or progressive muscle relaxation can help to reduce hyperactivity and impulsivity by promoting relaxation and reducing stress.

5. Seeking social support: Seeking support from family, friends, or support groups can be helpful in managing impulsivity and hyperactivity. Support can involve encouragement, understanding, and practical help with managing daily tasks.

TIME-MANAGEMENT STRATEGIES

Effective time management is critical for individuals with Adult ADHD to improve their productivity, reduce stress, and stay organized. Here are some time-management strategies that can be helpful:

1. Establishing a daily routine: Setting a daily routine can help individuals with Adult ADHD to stay on track and reduce the likelihood of forgetting important tasks or appointments. This routine should include time for work, leisure activities, and self-care.
2. Using a planner: A planner can be a useful tool for individuals with Adult ADHD to keep track of tasks and appointments. A planner can include both short-term and long-term goals, as well as reminders for upcoming events.
3. Prioritizing tasks: Prioritizing tasks based on their level of importance and urgency can help individuals with Adult ADHD to stay on track and reduce the likelihood of becoming overwhelmed. This can involve using a to-do list or breaking tasks down into smaller parts.
4. Setting goals: Setting achievable goals can help individuals with Adult ADHD to stay motivated and focused. Goals should be specific, measurable, and realistic, and should include a timeline for completion.
5. Avoiding procrastination: Procrastination can be a common challenge for individuals with Adult ADHD. Strategies to avoid procrastination can include breaking tasks down into smaller parts, setting a timer, and working in short bursts.

Effective time management requires a combination of environmental and behavioral strategies. It may take some trial and error to find the strategies that work best for each individual, but with persistence and patience, it is possible to improve time management skills and reduce stress.

ORGANIZATIONAL STRATEGIES

Organizational strategies can be helpful for individuals with Adult ADHD to reduce clutter, stay focused, and improve productivity. Here are some organizational strategies that can be effective:

1. Decluttering: Decluttering can help to reduce distractions and improve focus. This can involve getting rid of unnecessary items, organizing items into categories, and creating designated spaces for frequently used items.
2. Creating a system for organizing tasks: Creating a system for organizing tasks can help individuals with Adult ADHD to stay on track and reduce the likelihood of forgetting important tasks. This can involve using a to-do list, breaking tasks down into smaller parts, and setting reminders for upcoming events.
3. Using visual aids: Visual aids can be a helpful tool for individuals with Adult ADHD to stay organized and reduce clutter. This can involve using labels, color-coding items, and creating a visual schedule.
4. Developing a filing system: Developing a filing system can help individuals with Adult ADHD to keep important documents and papers organized. This can involve creating designated folders for different types of documents, such as bills, medical records, and important papers.
5. Simplifying daily tasks: Simplifying daily tasks can help individuals with Adult ADHD to reduce overwhelm and improve productivity. This can involve breaking tasks

down into smaller parts, focusing on one task at a time, and taking breaks as needed.

Organizational strategies require a combination of environmental and behavioral strategies. It may take some trial and error to find the strategies that work best for each individual, but with persistence and patience, it is possible to improve organizational skills and reduce stress.

COPING WITH EMOTIONS AND STRESS

Emotional dysregulation and stress can be common challenges for individuals with Adult ADHD. Coping strategies for managing emotions and stress can include the following:

1. Mindfulness: Mindfulness techniques, such as meditation and deep breathing, can help individuals with Adult ADHD to stay present and calm in the face of stress.
2. Exercise: Regular exercise can help to reduce stress and improve mood. This can involve engaging in activities such as walking, yoga, or strength training.
3. Cognitive-behavioral therapy: Cognitive-behavioral therapy (CBT) can be an effective treatment for individuals with Adult ADHD who struggle with emotional dysregulation. CBT can help individuals to identify negative thought patterns and develop strategies for managing their emotions.
4. Self-care: Engaging in self-care activities, such as getting enough sleep, eating a healthy diet, and engaging in hobbies, can help individuals with Adult ADHD to reduce stress and improve their overall well-being.
5. Social support: Building a strong social support network can be helpful for individuals with Adult ADHD to manage stress and regulate emotions. This can involve reaching out to friends and family members, joining a support group, or seeking professional help.

Overall, coping with emotions and stress requires a combination of environmental and behavioral strategies. It may take some trial and error to find the strategies that work best for each individual, but with persistence and patience, it is possible to improve emotional regulation and reduce stress.

STRATEGIES FOR PERSONAL GROWTH AND DEVELOPMENT

Personal growth and development is an ongoing process that involves learning, self-reflection, and intentional actions to improve oneself. Here are some strategies for personal growth and development:

BUILDING SELF-AWARENESS AND SELF-ACCEPTANCE

Building self-awareness and self-acceptance is a key component of personal growth and development. Here are some strategies for developing self-awareness and self-acceptance:

1. Practice mindfulness: Mindfulness involves paying attention to present moment experiences without judgment. By practicing mindfulness, you can become more aware of your thoughts, emotions, and bodily sensations, which can help increase self-awareness and self-acceptance.
2. Keep a journal: Writing down your thoughts and feelings in a journal can help increase self-awareness and self-acceptance. Regular journaling can help you identify patterns in your thoughts and emotions, which can help you better understand yourself.
3. Seek feedback: Seeking feedback from others can provide valuable insights into your strengths and weaknesses. Ask friends, family, or colleagues for feedback on your behavior or performance.
4. Identify your values: Identifying your values can help you better understand what is important to you and guide your

behavior. Reflect on what you value most in life and consider how your actions align with those values.
5. Challenge negative self-talk: Negative self-talk can undermine self-awareness and self-acceptance. When you notice negative self-talk, challenge it by replacing it with more positive and affirming thoughts.
6. Practice self-compassion: Self-compassion involves treating yourself with kindness and understanding, particularly in moments of difficulty or failure. By practicing self-compassion, you can increase self-acceptance and reduce self-criticism.
7. Seek support: Building self-awareness and self-acceptance can be challenging. Seek support from a therapist, coach, or trusted friend to help you navigate the process.

LEVERAGING STRENGTHS AND INTERESTS

Leveraging strengths and interests is an important part of personal growth and development. By identifying and utilizing our strengths and interests, we can increase our motivation, engagement, and overall well-being. Here are some strategies for leveraging strengths and interests:

1. Identify your strengths: Reflect on your past successes and accomplishments to identify your strengths. You can also take a strengths assessment, such as the Clifton Strengths assessment, to gain insight into your natural talents.
2. Use your strengths: Once you have identified your strengths, look for ways to use them in your personal and professional life. For example, if you have strong communication skills, you may enjoy leading meetings or presenting ideas to others.
3. Develop new skills: Building on your strengths can help you develop new skills and knowledge. Seek out opportunities to learn and grow in areas related to your strengths and interests.

4. Pursue hobbies and interests: Engaging in hobbies and interests can help increase motivation, engagement, and overall well-being. Look for opportunities to pursue your hobbies and interests in your personal and professional life.
5. Set goals aligned with your strengths: Set goals that align with your strengths and interests to increase motivation and engagement. For example, if you have a passion for writing, you may set a goal to write a book or start a blog.
6. Seek opportunities to use your strengths: Look for opportunities to use your strengths in your personal and professional life. For example, if you have strong leadership skills, you may seek out leadership roles in your community or at work.

DEVELOPING NEW SKILLS AND HABITS

Developing new skills and habits is an important part of personal growth and development. Here are some strategies for developing new skills and habits:

1. Set goals: Start by setting clear goals for the skills and habits you want to develop. Make sure your goals are specific, measurable, and realistic.
2. Create a plan: Once you have set your goals, create a plan for how you will achieve them. Break down your goals into smaller, manageable steps and set deadlines for each step.
3. Find resources: Identify the resources you need to develop your new skills and habits. This may include books, online courses, mentors, or coaches.
4. Practice regularly: Consistent practice is key to developing new skills and habits. Make time in your schedule for regular practice and commit to sticking to your plan.
5. Get feedback: Seek feedback from others to help you improve your skills and habits. This can be from a mentor,

coach, or friend who has expertise in the area you are developing.
6. Be patient and persistent: Developing new skills and habits takes time and effort. Be patient with yourself and celebrate small successes along the way. Stay persistent, even when progress is slow.
7. Hold yourself accountable: Hold yourself accountable for your progress by tracking your progress, evaluating your performance regularly, and adjusting your plan as needed.

STRATEGIES FOR BUILDING RELATIONSHIPS

Building positive relationships is essential for personal growth and development. Here are some strategies for building relationships:

1. Be genuine and authentic: Be yourself and show authenticity in your interactions with others. People are more likely to connect with you when they sense that you are genuine.
2. Practice active listening: Pay attention to what others are saying and try to understand their perspectives. Practice active listening by asking clarifying questions and repeating back what you hear.
3. Show empathy and understanding: Show empathy and understanding by putting yourself in others' shoes and trying to understand their feelings and perspectives. This can help build trust and rapport in your relationships.
4. Be respectful and considerate: Treat others with respect and consideration. Avoid behaviors that could be perceived as rude, dismissive, or disrespectful.
5. Practice open and honest communication: Communicate openly and honestly with others. Avoid gossip, lies, or withholding information that could damage trust in your relationships.
6. Find common ground: Identify common interests or goals that you share with others. This can help you build

stronger connections and find opportunities to collaborate.
7. Be supportive: Show support and encouragement for others. Celebrate their successes and provide a listening ear during difficult times.
8. Invest time and energy: Building relationships takes time and effort. Be willing to invest time and energy into building and maintaining relationships with others.

Remember that building positive relationships is an ongoing process that requires effort and commitment. By being genuine, practicing active listening, showing empathy and understanding, being respectful and considerate, practicing open and honest communication, finding common ground, being supportive, and investing time and energy, you can build strong and meaningful relationships that will contribute to your personal growth and development.

MINDFULNESS AND SELF-CARE

Mindfulness and self-care are important practices for promoting personal growth and well-being. Here are some strategies for incorporating mindfulness and self-care into your daily life:

1. Practice meditation: Meditation is a mindfulness practice that can help reduce stress, improve focus, and promote relaxation. Find a quiet place to sit or lie down and focus on your breath, letting go of any distracting thoughts.
2. Take breaks: Take regular breaks throughout the day to give yourself time to recharge. This can include taking a short walk, stretching, or simply taking a few deep breaths.
3. Practice self-compassion: Be kind and compassionate towards yourself. Recognize that you are only human and give yourself permission to make mistakes.
4. Engage in physical activity: Regular exercise can help improve your mood, reduce stress, and promote overall

well-being. Find an activity that you enjoy and make it a regular part of your routine.
5. Connect with nature: Spending time in nature can help reduce stress and promote relaxation. Take a walk in the park, spend time gardening, or simply sit outside and enjoy the fresh air.
6. Set boundaries: Set boundaries to protect your time and energy. Learn to say no to commitments that are not essential to your well-being.
7. Practice gratitude: Take time each day to reflect on the things you are grateful for. This can help shift your focus to the positive aspects of your life and improve your mood.
8. Engage in hobbies and interests: Make time for activities that bring you joy and fulfillment. This can help reduce stress and promote overall well-being.

Remember that mindfulness and self-care practices are personal and can vary from person to person. It's important to find strategies that work for you and incorporate them into your daily routine. By practicing mindfulness and self-care, you can improve your overall well-being and promote personal growth.

COPING WITH WORK AND SCHOOL

Coping with work and school can be challenging for individuals with Adult ADHD (Attention Deficit Hyperactivity Disorder), but there are strategies that can help. Here are some tips for coping with work and school:

STRATEGIES FOR SUCCESS IN THE WORKPLACE

Individuals with Adult ADHD (Attention Deficit Hyperactivity Disorder) may face unique challenges in the workplace, but there are strategies that can help them succeed. Here are some tips for success in the workplace:

1. Find a job that suits your strengths: Some jobs may be better suited for individuals with ADHD, such as those that involve fast-paced environments, multitasking, or creativity. Finding a job that aligns with your strengths can increase job satisfaction and success.
2. Communicate with your employer: Open communication with your employer can be helpful in managing symptoms of ADHD. Discussing your strengths and weaknesses and working together to develop a plan for success can lead to greater productivity and job satisfaction.
3. Break tasks into smaller steps: Large projects can be overwhelming for individuals with ADHD. Breaking tasks into smaller, manageable steps can make them more approachable and increase the likelihood of success.
4. Use tools and technology: Technology can be a helpful tool for individuals with ADHD. Tools such as timers,

alarms, and calendars can help with time management and organization, and software and apps can assist with task management and prioritization.
5. Create a structured routine: Creating a structured routine can help individuals with ADHD stay organized and on track. This can include setting specific times for tasks, prioritizing responsibilities, and using tools such as calendars, to-do lists, and reminders.
6. Minimize distractions: Minimizing distractions in the workplace can help individuals with ADHD stay focused. This can include using noise-cancelling headphones, turning off notifications, and finding a quiet space to work.
7. Take breaks: Taking regular breaks can help individuals with ADHD stay focused and avoid burnout. This can include short breaks throughout the day to stretch, move around, or engage in a calming activity.
8. Seek support: Support from friends, family, and mental health professionals can be helpful for individuals with ADHD. Therapy can provide strategies for coping with symptoms and managing stress, and support groups can provide a sense of community and validation.

NAVIGATING CAREER CHALLENGES WITH ADULT ADHD

Navigating career challenges with Adult ADHD (Attention Deficit Hyperactivity Disorder) can be difficult, but there are strategies that can help. Here are some tips for navigating career challenges with ADHD:

1. Know your strengths and limitations: Understanding your strengths and limitations can help you choose a career that aligns with your abilities and can help you succeed. It can

also help you identify areas where you may need additional support.
2. Communicate with your employer: Open communication with your employer can be helpful in managing symptoms of ADHD. Discussing your strengths and weaknesses and working together to develop a plan for success can lead to greater productivity and job satisfaction.
3. Seek accommodations: Individuals with ADHD may be eligible for accommodations at work, such as extended time on tasks, breaks during the workday, or a quiet workspace. It's important to talk to employers or disability services to explore available accommodations.
4. Use tools and technology: Technology can be a helpful tool for individuals with ADHD. Tools such as timers, alarms, and calendars can help with time management and organization, and software and apps can assist with task management and prioritization.
5. Create a structured routine: Creating a structured routine can help individuals with ADHD stay organized and on track. This can include setting specific times for tasks, prioritizing responsibilities, and using tools such as calendars, to-do lists, and reminders.
6. Minimize distractions: Minimizing distractions in the workplace can help individuals with ADHD stay focused. This can include using noise-cancelling headphones, turning off notifications, and finding a quiet space to work.
7. Take breaks: Taking regular breaks can help individuals with ADHD stay focused and avoid burnout. This can include short breaks throughout the day to stretch, move around, or engage in a calming activity.
8. Seek support: Support from friends, family, and mental health professionals can be helpful for individuals with ADHD. Therapy can provide strategies for coping with symptoms and managing stress, and support groups can provide a sense of community and validation.

9. Manage stress: Stress can exacerbate symptoms of ADHD. It's important to find healthy ways to manage stress, such as exercise, mindfulness practices, or talking to a therapist.

STRATEGIES FOR ACADEMIC SUCCESS WITH ADULT ADHD

Academic success with Adult ADHD (Attention Deficit Hyperactivity Disorder) can be challenging, but there are strategies that can help. Here are some tips for academic success with ADHD:

1. Create a structured routine: Creating a structured routine can help individuals with ADHD stay organized and on track. This can include setting specific times for studying, prioritizing responsibilities, and using tools such as calendars, to-do lists, and reminders.
2. Minimize distractions: Minimizing distractions while studying can help individuals with ADHD stay focused. This can include finding a quiet space to study, turning off notifications, and using noise-cancelling headphones.
3. Break tasks into smaller steps: Large projects can be overwhelming for individuals with ADHD. Breaking tasks into smaller, manageable steps can make them more approachable and increase the likelihood of success.
4. Use tools and technology: Technology can be a helpful tool for individuals with ADHD. Tools such as timers, alarms, and calendars can help with time management and organization, and software and apps can assist with task management and prioritization.
5. Seek accommodations: Individuals with ADHD may be eligible for accommodations at school, such as extended time on tests or assignments, a quiet space to take tests, or note-taking support. It's important to talk to disability

services or a counselor to explore available accommodations.
6. Take breaks: Taking regular breaks can help individuals with ADHD stay focused and avoid burnout. This can include short breaks throughout the day to stretch, move around, or engage in a calming activity.
7. Use active studying techniques: Active studying techniques, such as using flashcards, summarizing material, or teaching concepts to someone else, can help individuals with ADHD engage with the material and improve retention.
8. Prioritize self-care: Prioritizing self-care, such as getting enough sleep, eating a balanced diet, and exercising regularly, can help individuals with ADHD manage symptoms and improve academic performance.
9. Seek support: Support from friends, family, and mental health professionals can be helpful for individuals with ADHD. Therapy can provide strategies for coping with symptoms and managing stress, and support groups can provide a sense of community and validation.

In summary, strategies for academic success with Adult ADHD require creating a structured routine, minimizing distractions, breaking tasks into smaller steps, using tools and technology, seeking accommodations, taking breaks, using active studying techniques, prioritizing self-care, and seeking support. By implementing these strategies, individuals with ADHD can manage their symptoms and achieve academic success.

MANAGING ADHD IN COLLEGE AND GRADUATE SCHOOL

Managing ADHD in college and graduate school can be challenging, but there are strategies that can help. Here are some tips for managing ADHD in higher education:

1. Create a structured routine: Creating a structured routine can help individuals with ADHD stay organized and on track. This can include setting specific times for studying, prioritizing responsibilities, and using tools such as calendars, to-do lists, and reminders.
2. Minimize distractions: Minimizing distractions while studying can help individuals with ADHD stay focused. This can include finding a quiet space to study, turning off notifications, and using noise-cancelling headphones.
3. Break tasks into smaller steps: Large projects can be overwhelming for individuals with ADHD. Breaking tasks into smaller, manageable steps can make them more approachable and increase the likelihood of success.
4. Use tools and technology: Technology can be a helpful tool for individuals with ADHD. Tools such as timers, alarms, and calendars can help with time management and organization, and software and apps can assist with task management and prioritization.
5. Seek accommodations: Individuals with ADHD may be eligible for accommodations at school, such as extended time on tests or assignments, a quiet space to take tests, or note-taking support. It's important to talk to disability services or a counselor to explore available accommodations.
6. Take breaks: Taking regular breaks can help individuals with ADHD stay focused and avoid burnout. This can include short breaks throughout the day to stretch, move around, or engage in a calming activity.
7. Use active studying techniques: Active studying techniques, such as using flashcards, summarizing material, or teaching concepts to someone else, can help individuals with ADHD engage with the material and improve retention.
8. Prioritize self-care: Prioritizing self-care, such as getting enough sleep, eating a balanced diet, and exercising

regularly, can help individuals with ADHD manage symptoms and improve academic performance.
9. Seek support: Support from friends, family, and mental health professionals can be helpful for individuals with ADHD. Therapy can provide strategies for coping with symptoms and managing stress, and support groups can provide a sense of community and validation.

In addition to these strategies, it's important for individuals with ADHD to communicate with professors and seek academic and emotional support when needed. Many colleges and universities have resources for students with ADHD, such as tutoring, counseling services, and study skills workshops.

Overall, managing ADHD in college and graduate school requires a combination of strategies, accommodations, and support. By implementing these strategies and seeking support when needed, individuals with ADHD can achieve academic success and improve overall well-being.

ACCOMMODATIONS AND RESOURCES FOR ADULT ADHD IN THE WORKPLACE AND ACADEMIC SETTINGS

Accommodations and resources for Adult ADHD in the workplace and academic settings can help individuals with ADHD manage symptoms and improve performance. Here are some common accommodations and resources available:

In the Workplace:

- Flexible work schedule: This can include flexible start and end times, as well as flexible break times throughout the day.
- Noise-cancelling headphones: This can help individuals with ADHD minimize distractions in a busy workplace.

- Written instructions and checklists: Providing written instructions and checklists can help individuals with ADHD stay organized and on track.
- Breaks and frequent feedback: Taking regular breaks and receiving frequent feedback can help individuals with ADHD manage stress and stay focused.
- Technology tools: Technology tools such as organizational software, reminders, and timers can help individuals with ADHD manage time and prioritize tasks.
- Job coaching: Job coaching can provide guidance and support for individuals with ADHD in navigating workplace challenges and managing symptoms.

In Academic Settings:

- Extended time on exams: This can help individuals with ADHD manage test-taking anxiety and complete exams without feeling rushed.
- Note-taking support: This can include access to notes from a classmate or a note-taking app that can assist in capturing and organizing information.
- Quiet testing environment: A quiet environment can help individuals with ADHD minimize distractions during exams.
- Tutoring and academic coaching: This can provide additional support in understanding and retaining course material.
- Accommodations for assignments: Accommodations may include extended deadlines, reduced workload, or breaking assignments into smaller components.
- Mental health services: Mental health services, such as counseling and therapy, can help individuals with ADHD manage symptoms and cope with academic stress.

It's important for individuals with ADHD to communicate with their employers or academic institutions about their needs and seek accommodations when necessary. Many workplaces and schools have resources and support available for individuals with ADHD. Seeking support from a mental health professional, such as a therapist or coach, can also provide additional strategies for managing symptoms and improving performance.

BUILDING STRONG RELATIONSHIPS AND SUPPORT NETWORKS

Building strong relationships and support networks can be crucial for individuals with Adult ADHD. Here are some strategies for building strong relationships and support networks:

1. Communication: Effective communication is key for building strong relationships. Individuals with Adult ADHD may benefit from being open and honest about their challenges and needs, and seeking feedback and support from others.
2. Seeking professional help: Professional help, such as therapy or coaching, can be helpful for individuals with Adult ADHD to improve communication and build stronger relationships.
3. Joining a support group: Joining a support group can provide individuals with Adult ADHD with an opportunity to connect with others who share similar experiences and challenges.
4. Engaging in social activities: Engaging in social activities, such as volunteering, attending social events, or joining clubs or groups, can be helpful for individuals with Adult ADHD to build relationships and connect with others.
5. Building a routine: Building a routine can be helpful for individuals with Adult ADHD to manage their time and reduce stress, which can improve their ability to build and maintain relationships.

Overall, building strong relationships and support networks requires a combination of environmental and behavioral strategies. It may take some trial and error to find the strategies that work best for each individual, but with persistence and patience, it is possible to build strong relationships and develop a supportive network.

COMMUNICATING ABOUT ADULT ADHD WITH LOVED ONES

Communicating about Adult ADHD with loved ones can be challenging, but it can also be an important step towards building stronger relationships and receiving the support that is needed. Here are some strategies for communicating about Adult ADHD with loved ones:

1. Education: Educating loved ones about Adult ADHD can help to reduce stigma and increase understanding. This can involve sharing information about the symptoms, causes, and treatments of Adult ADHD.
2. Self-awareness: Being self-aware about one's own ADHD symptoms and challenges can help to communicate more effectively with loved ones. This can involve identifying specific areas of difficulty, such as forgetfulness or impulsivity, and communicating these challenges in a clear and specific way.
3. Open and honest communication: Open and honest communication is key for building strong relationships. This can involve sharing one's feelings and experiences in a non-judgmental and respectful way, and listening to the perspectives of others.
4. Seeking feedback: Seeking feedback from loved ones can help to identify areas of strength and weakness, and develop strategies for managing ADHD symptoms. This can involve asking loved ones for specific feedback on

how ADHD symptoms impact the relationship, and working together to develop strategies for addressing these challenges.
5. Providing reassurance: Loved ones may have concerns or fears about Adult ADHD, and providing reassurance can help to reduce anxiety and build trust. This can involve acknowledging concerns, sharing personal successes, and expressing gratitude for the support and understanding of loved ones.

BUILDING SUPPORTIVE RELATIONSHIPS

Building supportive relationships can be essential for individuals with Adult ADHD. Here are some strategies for building supportive relationships:

1. Identify supportive individuals: It is important to identify individuals who are supportive, understanding, and accepting of ADHD. This may include family members, friends, co-workers, or mental health professionals.
2. Set boundaries: Setting boundaries can be helpful for maintaining supportive relationships. This can involve communicating one's needs and limits, and being assertive in asking for what is needed.
3. Practice effective communication: Effective communication is key for building supportive relationships. This may involve being honest and open about one's challenges and needs, listening actively, and expressing empathy and understanding.
4. Develop shared activities: Shared activities can be a great way to build and maintain supportive relationships. This may include participating in hobbies, joining social groups, or volunteering in the community.

5. Seek professional help: Seeking professional help, such as therapy or coaching, can be helpful for developing skills to build and maintain supportive relationships.
6. Practice self-care: Practicing self-care, such as exercise, meditation, or mindfulness, can be helpful for managing ADHD symptoms and reducing stress, which can improve one's ability to build and maintain supportive relationships.

Building supportive relationships requires effort, patience, and a willingness to be open and honest. By identifying supportive individuals, setting boundaries, practicing effective communication, developing shared activities, seeking professional help, and practicing self-care, it is possible to build and maintain supportive relationships that can provide essential support and understanding for individuals with Adult ADHD.

JOINING SUPPORT GROUPS

Joining a support group can be a valuable strategy for individuals with Adult ADHD. Here are some potential benefits of joining a support group:

1. Connection with others who understand: Joining a support group can provide a sense of connection with others who are experiencing similar challenges. This can help to reduce feelings of isolation and provide a sense of validation and understanding.
2. Information and education: Support groups can provide information and education about Adult ADHD, including symptoms, treatments, and coping strategies. This can help to increase understanding and develop skills to manage ADHD symptoms.
3. Emotional support: Support groups can provide emotional support, including empathy, validation, and a safe space

to share feelings and experiences. This can help to reduce stress, improve self-esteem, and build confidence.
4. Practical support: Support groups can provide practical support, such as advice, resources, and referrals. This can help to address practical challenges related to Adult ADHD, such as managing time, staying organized, and coping with stress.
5. Accountability: Support groups can provide a sense of accountability and motivation to manage ADHD symptoms and develop healthy habits. This can help to improve self-discipline and follow-through, which can lead to greater success in personal and professional life.

STRATEGIES FOR MANAGING CONFLICT

Managing conflict can be a challenge for individuals with Adult ADHD. Here are some strategies for managing conflict effectively:

1. Take a break: When conflict arises, it can be helpful to take a break and allow emotions to settle before attempting to resolve the issue. This can help to reduce emotional reactivity and increase clarity and perspective.
2. Practice active listening: Active listening involves fully listening to the other person's perspective without interrupting or judging. This can help to increase understanding and reduce defensiveness.
3. Use "I" statements: Using "I" statements, such as "I feel" or "I need," can help to express one's own feelings and needs without blaming or accusing the other person.
4. Focus on the issue, not the person: It can be helpful to focus on the specific issue at hand rather than attacking the person or making generalizations.

5. Seek common ground: Seeking common ground involves looking for areas of agreement and focusing on finding a solution that works for both parties.
6. Use humor: Using humor can help to reduce tension and increase perspective, but it is important to ensure that the humor is not used in a way that belittles or dismisses the other person's perspective.

COPING WITH SOCIAL ANXIETY

Social anxiety can be a common challenge for individuals with Adult ADHD. Here are some strategies for coping with social anxiety:

1. Practice relaxation techniques: Practicing relaxation techniques, such as deep breathing, meditation, or progressive muscle relaxation, can help to reduce physical symptoms of anxiety, such as muscle tension or rapid heartbeat.
2. Challenge negative thoughts: Social anxiety is often accompanied by negative thoughts and self-criticism. It can be helpful to challenge these thoughts by examining the evidence, considering alternative perspectives, and reframing negative thoughts in a more positive way.
3. Gradual exposure: Gradual exposure involves gradually exposing oneself to feared social situations, starting with less challenging situations and gradually working up to more challenging situations. This can help to build confidence and reduce avoidance behaviors.
4. Use social skills training: Social skills training can involve learning and practicing specific social skills, such as initiating conversations, making eye contact, or active listening. This can help to improve confidence and reduce anxiety in social situations.

5. Seek support: It can be helpful to seek support from a therapist, support group, or trusted friend or family member. This can provide a safe space to talk about social anxiety and develop strategies for coping.

NAVIGATING LIFE TRANSITIONS AND CHALLENGES

Navigating life transitions and challenges can be particularly challenging for individuals with ADHD. In this chapter, we will discuss some common challenges that individuals with ADHD may face during major life changes, and provide strategies for coping with these challenges. Navigating life transitions and challenges with ADHD can be challenging, but with the right strategies and support, it is possible to manage and thrive during major life changes.

ADHD AND LIFE TRANSITIONS

Life transitions can be particularly challenging for individuals with ADHD. This is because ADHD can affect various areas of life, including organization, time management, and impulsivity, which can all impact the ability to navigate transitions effectively.

Some common life transitions that may be particularly challenging for individuals with ADHD include:

- Starting College: College can be an exciting time, but it can also be overwhelming for individuals with ADHD. The transition to college life may involve living in a new environment, managing a more rigorous academic schedule, and meeting new people. Strategies for coping

with the transition to college may include developing a routine, seeking academic support, and using technology to manage time and tasks.
- Changing Jobs: Changing jobs can also be a challenging transition for individuals with ADHD. The transition to a new job may involve learning new skills, adjusting to a new work environment, and managing new responsibilities. Strategies for coping with the transition to a new job may include seeking support from a career counselor or mentor, developing a routine for managing work tasks, and breaking down job responsibilities into manageable steps.
- Getting Married: Marriage is a major life transition that can be particularly challenging for individuals with ADHD. The transition to marriage may involve adjusting to a new living situation, managing finances, and navigating the complexities of a new relationship. Strategies for coping with the transition to marriage may include seeking support from a therapist or support group, practicing effective communication skills, and using technology to manage shared tasks and responsibilities.

The key to successfully navigating life transitions with ADHD is to be proactive and develop strategies that work for you. Seeking support from friends, family, and professionals can also be helpful in managing the challenges that may arise during life transitions.

MANAGING ADHD DURING MAJOR LIFE CHANGES

Managing ADHD during major life changes can be particularly challenging, as these changes can disrupt routines and trigger symptoms of ADHD. Some common major life changes that may require additional support for individuals with ADHD include:

1. Moving: Moving to a new home or city can be particularly challenging for individuals with ADHD, as it involves a disruption of routine and a need to establish new routines. To manage ADHD during a move, it can be helpful to plan ahead and break down tasks into smaller, manageable steps. It may also be helpful to use organizational tools such as checklists, calendars, and labeling systems to keep track of tasks and manage the move.
2. Starting a new job: Starting a new job can also be a significant change that can be particularly challenging for individuals with ADHD. To manage ADHD during the transition to a new job, it may be helpful to communicate with your employer about your ADHD and any accommodations that may be helpful. It may also be helpful to break down job responsibilities into manageable steps and to develop a routine for managing work tasks.
3. Having a child: Having a child can also be a major life change that can be particularly challenging for individuals with ADHD. To manage ADHD during the transition to parenthood, it may be helpful to seek support from a therapist or support group, establish a routine for managing household tasks and responsibilities, and use technology to manage tasks and schedules.

Managing ADHD during major life changes involves being proactive and developing strategies that work for you. Seeking support from professionals, friends, and family can also be helpful in managing the challenges that may arise during major life changes.

COPING WITH CO-OCCURRING DISORDERS

Co-occurring disorders refer to the presence of two or more disorders or conditions in an individual. For individuals with ADHD, it is not uncommon to also have co-occurring disorders such as anxiety, depression, substance abuse, or learning disabilities. Coping with co-occurring disorders can be particularly challenging as the presence of one disorder can exacerbate symptoms of another. Here are some strategies for coping with co-occurring disorders:

1. Seek professional help: It is important to seek professional help if you suspect that you may have a co-occurring disorder. A mental health professional can help you identify any additional disorders or conditions and develop a treatment plan that addresses all of your needs.
2. Practice self-care: Practicing self-care is important for managing symptoms of ADHD and co-occurring disorders. This includes getting enough sleep, eating a healthy diet, and engaging in regular exercise. It is also important to engage in activities that bring you joy and help you relax, such as meditation or yoga.
3. Use medication and other treatments: Depending on the co-occurring disorder, medication and other treatments may be helpful in managing symptoms. It is important to work with a healthcare professional to determine the best course of treatment for your individual needs.
4. Join support groups: Joining support groups for individuals with ADHD and co-occurring disorders can be helpful in managing symptoms and finding support. Support groups can provide a safe space to share experiences, learn coping strategies, and find support from others who are going through similar experiences.
5. Practice mindfulness: Mindfulness practices such as meditation or deep breathing exercises can be helpful in managing symptoms of ADHD and co-occurring disorders. These practices can help you stay present and

focused, manage anxiety and stress, and improve overall well-being.

Coping with co-occurring disorders involves seeking professional help, practicing self-care, using medication and other treatments, joining support groups, and practicing mindfulness. It is important to remember that co-occurring disorders are common, and with the right treatment and support, it is possible to manage symptoms and improve overall quality of life.

COPING WITH FINANCIAL CHALLENGES

For individuals with ADHD, managing finances can be a challenging task. It is not uncommon for individuals with ADHD to struggle with impulse control and distractibility, which can lead to financial difficulties. Here are some strategies for coping with financial challenges:

1. Create a budget: Creating a budget is an important first step in managing finances. This involves tracking income and expenses, and creating a plan for how money will be spent each month. There are many online tools and apps available to help create and track a budget.
2. Set financial goals: Setting financial goals can provide motivation and help you stay focused on managing finances. This might include saving for a specific purchase or paying off debt.
3. Automate bill payments: Automating bill payments can help ensure that bills are paid on time, which can help avoid late fees and damage to credit scores.
4. Limit access to credit: For individuals with ADHD, impulsivity can lead to overspending and accumulating debt. It may be helpful to limit access to credit, such as by canceling credit cards or placing a freeze on credit reports.
5. Seek financial counseling: Financial counseling can be helpful in developing strategies for managing finances

and reducing debt. This may involve working with a financial advisor or counselor to create a debt management plan.
6. Develop organizational systems: Developing organizational systems for managing finances, such as keeping receipts and bills in a designated location, can be helpful in reducing stress and avoiding missed payments.
7. Practice mindfulness: Mindfulness practices, such as deep breathing exercises or meditation, can be helpful in managing impulsivity and reducing stress related to financial challenges.

coping with financial challenges involves creating a budget, setting financial goals, automating bill payments, limiting access to credit, seeking financial counseling, developing organizational systems, and practicing mindfulness. By implementing these strategies, individuals with ADHD can successfully manage their finances and improve overall financial well-being.

PLANNING FOR THE FUTURE WITH ADULT ADHD

Planning for the future can be challenging for individuals with ADHD, who often struggle with impulsivity, distractibility, and difficulty with organization. However, there are strategies that can help individuals with ADHD plan for the future and achieve their goals.

- Set realistic goals: It is important to set goals that are achievable and realistic. This might involve breaking down larger goals into smaller, more manageable steps.
- Prioritize goals: Prioritizing goals can help individuals with ADHD focus their energy and attention on the most important goals. This might involve identifying short-

term and long-term goals, and creating a plan for achieving them.
- Develop a routine: Developing a routine can help individuals with ADHD stay organized and focused on their goals. This might involve creating a daily or weekly schedule, and breaking down tasks into smaller steps.
- Use tools and technology: There are many tools and technologies available that can help individuals with ADHD plan and organize their future. This might include using a planner, setting reminders, or using apps to track progress and stay motivated.
- Seek support: It can be helpful to seek support from family, friends, or a mental health professional when planning for the future. This might involve discussing goals with a trusted friend or family member, or working with a therapist to develop strategies for achieving goals.
- Practice self-care: Self-care is important for managing ADHD symptoms and staying focused on future goals. This might involve engaging in activities that reduce stress, such as exercise or meditation, or taking breaks when feeling overwhelmed.
- Stay positive: Maintaining a positive attitude and focusing on strengths and successes can help individuals with ADHD stay motivated and achieve their goals.

Overall, planning for the future with ADHD involves setting realistic goals, prioritizing goals, developing a routine, using tools and technology, seeking support, practicing self-care, and maintaining a positive attitude. By implementing these strategies, individuals with ADHD can successfully plan for the future and achieve their goals.

LIVING YOUR BEST LIFE WITH ADULT ADHD

Living your best life with adult ADHD can be challenging, but it is possible with the right strategies and support. Here are some tips for living your best life with adult ADHD:

CELEBRATING SUCCESSES

Celebrating successes is an important part of personal growth and development. Celebrating your successes can help boost your self-esteem, increase motivation, and provide a sense of accomplishment. Here are some tips for celebrating your successes:

1. Acknowledge your accomplishments: Take time to acknowledge your accomplishments and give yourself credit for your hard work.
2. Reflect on your progress: Reflect on your progress and how far you've come. This can help you appreciate your journey and feel proud of your accomplishments.

3. Share your success with others: Share your success with friends, family, or a supportive community. This can help you feel validated and increase your sense of connection.
4. Treat yourself: Treat yourself to something special as a reward for your hard work. This can be anything from a small indulgence to a bigger celebration.
5. Set new goals: Use your success as a springboard for setting new goals and continuing to grow and develop.

Remember that celebrating successes doesn't have to be extravagant or expensive. It's about acknowledging and appreciating your accomplishments, no matter how big or small they may be. By taking the time to celebrate your successes, you can increase your motivation and sense of self-worth, which can contribute to your overall well-being and personal growth.

STRATEGIES FOR MAINTAINING PROGRESS

Maintaining progress is key to achieving long-term personal growth and development. Here are some strategies for maintaining progress:

1. Set realistic goals: Set goals that are realistic and achievable. This can help you avoid becoming overwhelmed and feeling discouraged.
2. Create a plan: Create a plan for achieving your goals and breaking them down into smaller, manageable steps. This can help you stay on track and measure your progress.
3. Track your progress: Keep track of your progress and celebrate your successes along the way. This can help you stay motivated and build momentum.
4. Stay flexible: Be open to adjusting your goals and plans as needed. Life is unpredictable, and sometimes

circumstances change. Being flexible can help you adapt to these changes and continue making progress.
5. Practice self-care: Take care of yourself by getting enough sleep, eating well, and engaging in activities that bring you joy. This can help you maintain your energy and motivation.
6. Seek support: Seek support from friends, family, or a therapist who understands your goals and can help you stay accountable.
7. Stay positive: Focus on the positive aspects of your progress and avoid getting bogged down by setbacks or challenges. Maintaining a positive mindset can help you stay motivated and continue making progress.

Remember that maintaining progress is a lifelong process, and it's okay to take things one step at a time. By setting realistic goals, creating a plan, tracking your progress, and practicing self-care, you can maintain your momentum and achieve long-term personal growth and development.

LIVING WITH INTENTION AND PURPOSE

Living with intention and purpose involves living your life according to your values and goals. It means being intentional about your actions and decisions, and striving to live a fulfilling life. Here are some strategies for living with intention and purpose:

1. Identify your values: Take the time to identify your core values and what matters most to you. This can help guide your decisions and actions.
2. Set meaningful goals: Set goals that are aligned with your values and that have a sense of purpose. This can help you stay motivated and focused on what matters most to you.
3. Create a vision for your life: Create a vision for your life that aligns with your values and goals. This can help you stay focused on the big picture and avoid getting caught up in day-to-day distractions.

4. Practice mindfulness: Practice being present in the moment and focusing on the task at hand. This can help you stay focused and avoid distractions.
5. Prioritize self-care: Take care of yourself by getting enough sleep, eating well, and engaging in activities that bring you joy. This can help you maintain your energy and motivation.
6. Surround yourself with supportive people: Surround yourself with people who support your values and goals and who encourage you to be your best self.
7. Take action: Take action towards your goals and values on a daily basis. This can help you feel a sense of accomplishment and purpose.

Remember that living with intention and purpose is a lifelong journey, and it's okay to make mistakes along the way. By identifying your values, setting meaningful goals, and taking intentional action, you can create a fulfilling life that is aligned with your deepest desires and aspirations.

STAYING ENGAGED AND MOTIVATED

Staying engaged and motivated can be challenging, especially when facing setbacks or obstacles. However, there are strategies that can help you stay engaged and motivated on a daily basis. Here are some tips:

1. Break down big goals into small, achievable steps: Instead of focusing on a large, intimidating goal, break it down into smaller, achievable steps. This can help you stay motivated and feel a sense of accomplishment as you complete each step.
2. Set clear deadlines: Setting deadlines can help you stay focused and accountable. Make sure your deadlines are realistic and achievable.

3. Use positive self-talk: Replace negative self-talk with positive affirmations. This can help you stay motivated and focused on your goals.
4. Celebrate successes: Celebrate your successes, no matter how small. This can help you stay motivated and build momentum.
5. Stay organized: Use a planner or calendar to stay organized and keep track of your progress. This can help you stay on track and avoid feeling overwhelmed.
6. Take breaks: Take regular breaks to rest and recharge. This can help you maintain your energy and motivation.
7. Find inspiration: Surround yourself with people who inspire you or engage in activities that motivate you. This can help you stay engaged and motivated on a daily basis.

Remember that staying engaged and motivated is a process that requires consistent effort and commitment. By breaking down big goals into achievable steps, setting clear deadlines, using positive self-talk, celebrating successes, staying organized, taking breaks, and finding inspiration, you can maintain your momentum and achieve your goals.

CONTINUING TO GROW AND LEARN

Continuing to grow and learn is an important aspect of personal development and can help you lead a fulfilling life. Here are some strategies for continuing to grow and learn:

1. Seek out new experiences: Try new things and step out of your comfort zone. This can help you learn new skills and gain new perspectives.
2. Set learning goals: Set specific learning goals for yourself, such as learning a new language or mastering a new skill. This can help you stay motivated and focused on your personal growth.
3. Read and educate yourself: Read books and articles on topics that interest you, or take online courses to learn new

skills. This can help you expand your knowledge and deepen your understanding of different subjects.
4. Reflect on your experiences: Reflect on your experiences and what you have learned from them. This can help you gain insight into your strengths and weaknesses and identify areas for growth.
5. Seek feedback: Ask for feedback from others, such as friends, family, or colleagues. This can help you identify areas for improvement and gain new perspectives on your strengths and weaknesses.
6. Connect with others: Connect with people who share your interests or who have expertise in areas you want to learn more about. This can help you learn from others and expand your knowledge and skills.
7. Embrace challenges: Embrace challenges and view them as opportunities for growth and learning. This can help you develop resilience and a growth mindset.

Remember that personal growth and learning is a lifelong journey. By seeking out new experiences, setting learning goals, reading and educating yourself, reflecting on your experiences, seeking feedback, connecting with others, and embracing challenges, you can continue to grow and learn throughout your life.

RESOURCES FOR ADULT ADHD

There are many resources available for adults with ADHD. Here are some examples:

1. National Institute of Mental Health: The National Institute of Mental Health (NIMH) provides information on ADHD symptoms, diagnosis, and treatment. Their website also includes resources for finding mental health services and clinical trials.
2. CHADD: CHADD (Children and Adults with Attention-Deficit/Hyperactivity Disorder) is a nonprofit organization that provides resources, support, and advocacy for individuals with ADHD and their families. Their website includes information on ADHD, support groups, and resources for finding mental health services.
3. Attention Deficit Disorder Association: The Attention Deficit Disorder Association (ADDA) provides resources and support for adults with ADHD. Their website includes information on ADHD, webinars, and resources for finding mental health services.
4. Understood: Understood is a nonprofit organization that provides resources and support for individuals with

learning and attention issues, including ADHD. Their website includes articles, videos, and tools for managing ADHD symptoms and improving academic and workplace performance.
5. The American Psychiatric Association: The American Psychiatric Association (APA) provides information on ADHD diagnosis and treatment. Their website includes resources for finding mental health services and educational materials for individuals with ADHD.
6. Online support groups: Online support groups can provide a sense of community and validation for individuals with ADHD. Websites such as ADDitude and Reddit have active communities of individuals with ADHD who share resources, strategies, and support.
7. Mental health professionals: Seeking support from a mental health professional, such as a therapist or coach, can provide personalized strategies for managing ADHD symptoms and improving overall well-being.

Overall, there are many resources available for adults with ADHD. It's important for individuals with ADHD to seek support and resources that fit their individual needs and preferences.

BOOKS AND WEBSITES

Here are some recommended books and websites for adults with ADHD:

Books:

1. "Driven to Distraction" by Edward Hallowell and John Ratey: This book provides an overview of ADHD and offers strategies for managing symptoms in different areas of life, including work, relationships, and daily routines.

2. "The ADHD Effect on Marriage" by Melissa Orlov: This book addresses the impact of ADHD on relationships and offers strategies for improving communication, managing conflict, and strengthening relationships.
3. "Taking Charge of Adult ADHD" by Russell A. Barkley: This book provides evidence-based strategies for managing ADHD symptoms, improving organization and time management, and reducing impulsivity.
4. "The Mindfulness Prescription for Adult ADHD" by Lidia Zylowska: This book offers mindfulness-based strategies for managing ADHD symptoms, reducing stress, and improving overall well-being.
5. "ADD-Friendly Ways to Organize Your Life" by Judith Kolberg and Kathleen Nadeau: This book offers practical tips and strategies for managing clutter, organizing spaces, and improving time management.

Websites:

1. ADDitude Magazine: ADDitude is an online magazine focused on ADHD, providing articles, webinars, and resources for managing ADHD symptoms, improving academic and workplace performance, and navigating relationships.
2. TotallyADD: TotallyADD is an online community for adults with ADHD, providing videos, articles, and resources for managing symptoms, improving organization and time management, and reducing stress.
3. ADHD Coaches Organization: The ADHD Coaches Organization provides a directory of ADHD coaches, as well as information on coaching and resources for managing ADHD symptoms.
4. HelpGuide: HelpGuide is a nonprofit organization providing articles and resources on mental health and well-being, including articles on managing ADHD symptoms and improving daily routines.

5. Psychology Today: Psychology today is an online magazine providing articles and resources on mental health and wellness. Their ADHD page provides articles on managing symptoms, improving relationships, and finding support.

It's important to note that while these resources can be helpful, it's important to consult with a mental health professional for personalized strategies and support in managing ADHD symptoms.

ORGANIZATIONS AND SUPPORT GROUPS

There are several organizations and support groups that provide resources and support for adults with ADHD. Here are some examples:

1. CHADD (Children and Adults with Attention-Deficit/Hyperactivity Disorder): CHADD is a nonprofit organization that provides resources, support, and advocacy for individuals with ADHD and their families. Their website includes information on ADHD, support groups, and resources for finding mental health services.
2. Attention Deficit Disorder Association (ADDA): ADDA provides resources and support for adults with ADHD. Their website includes information on ADHD, webinars, and resources for finding mental health services.
3. National Resource Center on ADHD: The National Resource Center on ADHD provides information and resources on ADHD for individuals with ADHD, their families, and healthcare providers.
4. The ADHD Collective: The ADHD Collective is a nonprofit organization that provides resources, support, and community for adults with ADHD. Their website includes articles, resources, and a community forum for individuals with ADHD.

5. TotallyADD: TotallyADD is an online community for adults with ADHD, providing videos, articles, and resources for managing symptoms, improving organization and time management, and reducing stress.
6. Adult ADHD NI: Adult ADHD NI is a support group based in Northern Ireland that provides resources and support for adults with ADHD.
7. Attention Deficit Disorder Resources: ADD Resources is a nonprofit organization that provides resources and support for individuals with ADHD and their families, including support groups, educational programs, and an online community.

These organizations and support groups can provide a sense of community and validation for individuals with ADHD, as well as resources and support for managing symptoms and improving well-being.

PROFESSIONAL HELP AND TREATMENT OPTIONS

Professional help and treatment options for adult ADHD can vary depending on the individual's specific needs and symptoms. Here are some options to consider:

1. Mental health professionals: Mental health professionals, such as psychiatrists, psychologists, and licensed therapists, can provide individual therapy, group therapy, and medication management for adult ADHD. These professionals can help individuals with ADHD develop coping strategies, manage symptoms, and improve overall functioning.
2. Medications: There are several medications that can be used to treat adult ADHD, including stimulants (such as Ritalin and Adderall) and non-stimulant medications (such as Strattera). These medications can help improve

focus, reduce impulsivity, and manage hyperactivity. It is important to work with a healthcare provider to determine the most appropriate medication and dosage for each individual.
3. Coaching: ADHD coaches are professionals who specialize in working with individuals with ADHD to help them develop strategies for managing symptoms, improving organization and time management, and setting and achieving goals. ADHD coaches can provide support and guidance to individuals with ADHD as they navigate work, school, and relationships.
4. Support groups: Support groups for adults with ADHD can provide a sense of community, validation, and support for individuals with ADHD. These groups may be led by mental health professionals, peer facilitators, or community organizations.
5. Alternative therapies: Some individuals with ADHD may find relief from symptoms through alternative therapies such as yoga, mindfulness, and acupuncture. It is important to work with a healthcare provider to determine the appropriateness and safety of these therapies.

It is important to note that seeking professional help for adult ADHD can be a complex and personal process. It may take time to find the right treatment and healthcare provider that works for each individual. It is important to be patient, persistent, and advocate for oneself in seeking appropriate care.

APPS AND TOOLS FOR MANAGING ADULT ADHD

There are several apps and tools that can help individuals with Adult ADHD manage their symptoms and improve their daily functioning. Here are some examples:

1. Headspace: Headspace is a meditation app that can help reduce stress and improve focus. It offers guided meditations and mindfulness exercises that can help individuals with ADHD manage symptoms and improve their ability to concentrate.
2. Trello: Trello is a project management tool that can help individuals with ADHD stay organized and on-task. It allows users to create to-do lists, set deadlines, and track progress on tasks and projects.
3. Forest: Forest is an app that helps individuals with ADHD stay focused and avoid distractions. It works by encouraging users to plant a virtual tree when they begin a task and providing rewards for staying focused.
4. Evernote: Evernote is a note-taking app that can help individuals with ADHD keep track of ideas, reminders, and important information. It allows users to create notes, to-do lists, and reminders, and syncs across devices.
5. MindMeister: MindMeister is a mind-mapping tool that can help individuals with ADHD organize their thoughts and ideas. It allows users to create visual diagrams that can help with brainstorming, planning, and problem-solving.
6. Habitica: Habitica is an app that turns productivity into a game. It allows users to track and reward progress on daily tasks and habits, encouraging positive habits and behavior changes.
7. Be Focused: Be Focused is a time-management app that can help individuals with ADHD stay on task and manage their time more effectively. It allows users to set timers for tasks and breaks, and provides a visual reminder of how much time is left for each task.

These apps and tools can provide support and structure for individuals with ADHD, helping to manage symptoms and improve daily functioning. It is important to note that these tools should be used in conjunction with other treatments and strategies, and that individuals with ADHD may need to experiment to find what works best for them.

ADDITIONAL RESOURCES FOR ADULT ADHD

In addition to professional help, books, websites, and apps, there are several other resources available for individuals with Adult ADHD. Here are a few examples:

1. ADHD coaches: ADHD coaches are professionals who specialize in working with individuals with ADHD to develop strategies for managing symptoms and improving functioning. They can provide support and guidance as individuals navigate work, school, and relationships.
2. Educational support services: Many colleges and universities offer educational support services for students with ADHD, such as tutoring, study skills workshops, and assistive technology.
3. Career services: Career services offices can provide guidance and resources for individuals with ADHD as they navigate career challenges and job search strategies.
4. Support groups: Support groups for adults with ADHD can provide a sense of community, validation, and support for individuals with ADHD. These groups may be led by mental health professionals, peer facilitators, or community organizations.
5. National Resource Center on ADHD: The National Resource Center on ADHD is a program of the Centers for Disease Control and Prevention (CDC) that provides information and resources on ADHD for individuals, families, and healthcare providers.
6. CHADD: CHADD (Children and Adults with Attention-Deficit/Hyperactivity Disorder) is a nonprofit organization that provides support and advocacy for individuals with ADHD and their families. They offer

resources such as webinars, conferences, and online support groups.
7. ADDitude Magazine: ADDitude Magazine is an online resource for individuals with ADHD and their families. It provides articles, webinars, and podcasts on topics related to ADHD, including treatment options, coping strategies, and personal stories.

These resources can provide additional support and guidance for individuals with Adult ADHD as they navigate daily challenges and seek to improve their functioning and quality of life.

CONCLUSION

In conclusion, Adult ADHD can present significant challenges in various aspects of life, including work, relationships, and daily functioning. However, with the right tools and strategies, individuals with ADHD can learn to manage their symptoms effectively and achieve their goals. This book has covered various topics related to Adult ADHD, including understanding the condition, the different types of ADHD, diagnosis and evaluation, medication and other treatments, coping strategies, building supportive relationships, and planning for the future. It is our hope that this book has provided valuable information and insights to individuals with ADHD and their loved ones, and that it serves as a useful resource for those looking to take charge of their ADHD and live fulfilling lives.

RECAP OF KEY CONCEPTS

Sure! Here's a recap of some key concepts covered in this book:

1. Adult ADHD is a neurodevelopmental disorder that affects attention, impulsivity, and hyperactivity.

2. There are three types of Adult ADHD: predominantly inattentive, predominantly hyperactive-impulsive, and combined.
3. A comprehensive evaluation is essential for an accurate diagnosis of Adult ADHD.
4. Medication and therapy are common treatments for Adult ADHD, but there are also alternative treatments available.
5. Coping strategies for Adult ADHD include time-management, organizational, and emotional regulation techniques.
6. Building supportive relationships and joining support groups can provide valuable resources and help with managing ADHD.
7. Life transitions and challenges can be especially difficult for individuals with ADHD, but with the right tools and strategies, it is possible to manage these challenges effectively.
8. Planning for the future, setting goals, and creating structure can help individuals with ADHD thrive and achieve their full potential.

THE IMPORTANCE OF TAKING CHARGE OF ADULT ADHD

Taking charge of Adult ADHD is crucial for several reasons. **Firstly,** it can significantly improve an individual's quality of life. Managing ADHD symptoms can help individuals feel more in control of their lives, reduce stress and anxiety, and improve relationships.

Secondly, untreated ADHD can have negative consequences, such as poor academic or work performance, difficulty maintaining relationships, and impulsive or risky behavior.

Thirdly, taking charge of Adult ADHD can lead to better long-term outcomes, such as improved career prospects, financial stability, and overall well-being.

Finally, by taking charge of Adult ADHD, individuals can also become advocates for themselves and others with ADHD. They can share their experiences and knowledge, help reduce stigma, and raise awareness about the condition.

Overall, taking charge of Adult ADHD is a critical step towards living a fulfilling and successful life, and it can benefit not just the individual with ADHD but also their loved ones and society as a whole.

Made in United States
North Haven, CT
29 August 2025